Of Water and Spirit

Youth
Discipleship
Journal

Deepening the Journey

A special thanks to the students of Graceland University's 2003 Youth Ministries winter term class who provided fresh ideas and suggestions: Kate Anderson, Shara Barbour, Julie Burks, Katie Carnahan, Quincy Clark, Chad Hensley, Meredith Hoffman, Chelsea Johnson, Abbey Riley, Karli Smith, Josh Sturgis, Jared Thatcher, Sarah Thatcher, Keely Thomas, Kyla Thrutchley, Jason Titus.

The scripture quotations contained herein are from the New Revised Standard Version Bible, copyright © 1989 by the Division of Christian Education of the National Council of the Churches of Christ in the U.S.A. and are used by permission. All rights reserved.

Scripture taken from the Holy Bible, NEW INTERNATIONAL VERSION®. Copyright © 1973, 1978, 1984 International Bible Society. All rights reserved throughout the world. Used by permission of International Bible Society.

References to the Holy Scriptures Inspired Version are indicated by IV. Community of Christ, Independence, Missouri.

The Book of Mormon, Revised Authorized Version, 1966, is used in this resource. Community of Christ, Independence, Missouri.

Effort has been made to trace all present copyright holders of the material used in this book. Any omission is unintentional and we will be pleased to correct any errors in future editions of this book.

Produced by Forefront Ministries
Community of Christ World Headquarters
Independence, Missouri

Project Management and Editor: Lynda Roberson
Authors: Dale Luffman, Sheryl Magee, Marge Nelson, Lynda Roberson, Diane Sadler
Editorial Team: Mary Jacks Dynes, Bob Kyser, Gary Logan
Cover Design: Chad Godfrey

Copyright ©2003 Community of Christ
Independence, Missouri

Distributed by Herald Publishing House
Printed in the United States of America
ISBN 0830910700

Contents

Resource Introduction 4

Session 1
God, Jesus, and the Holy Spirit 7

Session 2
Scriptures of the Church. 13

Session 3
Community of Christ: Then and Now 19

Session 4
Church Sacraments. 25

Session 5
Called to Serve the Lord 31

Session 6
A Disciple's Generous Response 37

Session 7
Discipleship in Community 43

Session 8
A Disciple's Call to Witness 49

Session 9
Deepening the Journey 55

Do You Want to Be Baptized? 61

Endnotes 62

Evaluation 63

Resource Introduction

Why would I use this resource?

- To deepen my personal commitment to the call of discipleship
- To better understand the Community of Christ faith tradition
- To make or renew my covenant with Jesus Christ
- To prepare for baptism and confirmation
- To discover new ways I can serve the Lord

What do I need to start?

- A copy of this resource
- An adult mentor
- A desire to deepen my discipleship journey
- A prayerful openness to the Holy Spirit
- Access to a Bible, Book of Mormon, and Doctrine and Covenants

Suggestions for Study Structure

- Weekly sessions with others
  - during church class
  - one night per week
  - at home with family

- Independent study with an adult mentor

- Camp/retreat
  - with youth and adult mentors
  - with youth and their families
  - as a whole congregation

What is an adult mentor and why do I need one?

The adult mentor is someone who is willing to commit to walk this journey of discovery with you. He/She will be available to discuss each session with you, help provide opportunities for experiences that will reinforce your discoveries, help you find answers to your questions and concerns, and pray with you and for you along the way.

Classes

If you are studying with a group, then one person will probably serve as a mentor to everyone in the class. In fact, they may be the one who initiates and encourages the study in the first place. He/She would be present at all class sessions and help to guide and facilitate discussion.

Family

If you are studying with your family, then one of your family members (parent, grandparent, aunt, or uncle) may serve as your mentor. However, another adult, possibly a priesthood member, may be asked to work with all of you. This resource can be beneficial to people of all ages.

Individual

If you are not able to study with a group, then ask an adult to be your mentor. You can work through the sessions in your own time, but make a point to discuss each session with your mentor before moving on to the next. It is best to meet in person, but if necessary, discussions can also take place by phone or e-mail.

Camp or Retreat

If you are working through this resource during a youth camp or retreat, then your mentor will probably be the camp pastor. If you are working through it during an intergenerational congregational retreat, then you will find that you have a multitude of mentors available for small group discussions and study.

My mentor is . . .

Write name of mentor(s) here.

After studying each session, you and your mentor should initial below to keep a record of your experience together. Sessions may be done in any order.

Mentor Sign-off

session

Mentor _____ 1
Youth _____

Mentor _____ 2
Youth _____

Mentor _____ 3
Youth _____

Mentor _____ 4
Youth _____

Mentor _____ 5
Youth _____

Mentor _____ 6
Youth _____

Mentor _____ 7
Youth _____

Mentor _____ 8
Youth _____

Mentor _____ 9
Youth _____

Why do I need my own book?

The book is your guide for thoughtful discussion and experiences. It is also your journal. Use the blank spaces to record and process your questions and responses as you work through the activities in each session.

A little info about the format . . .

- Each session is introduced with a graphic. Study the picture, then answer the question, "What does this image say to me?" in the space provided for image reflection.

- Next you will find an article that expresses the author's ideas about the topic. Read it, respond to the questions, and think for yourself. Where does it take you? What does it cause you to think, feel, or want to do?

- On the pages following the article you will find questions and activities that will help you delve deeper into your journey. Use the blank spaces in your journal to respond.

- Discuss your questions and thoughts with others, especially with your mentor.

- Pray as you study each session. Pray that God will fill your heart and mind with the Holy Spirit so that you may know the power of God in you.

What do you hope to get from this study?

Session Objectives

- To learn about the one eternal, living God

- To study one God in three persons: God the Parent, Jesus the Son, and the Holy Spirit

- To explore a relationship with God that is central to the life of a disciple

God, Jesus, and the Holy Spirit

IMAGE Reflection

1

We Begin with Spirit

We are spiritual beings living in a spiritual universe. The great Creator Spirit has called us into being. Our hunger is to know this Spirit as a Source of our true identity, the One in whom we find life, meaning, and joy. Our dreams, longings, visions, and callings have their origin in God. All spiritual stories and religious traditions begin out of transforming encounters with God's touch, voice, and light.

Despite the ways we misunderstand or distort such encounters as they pass through the filters of culture and ego, God continues to embrace, form, and heal us into beauty and wholeness. God's intentions toward us are good and glorious. We can trust God as the context in which we travel, the One calling to us.

Perhaps we have thought we could receive truth and preserve it as a marvelous thing that happened once upon a time. But formation—transformation—is ongoing. The Spirit continues to shape us into a people who embrace the redemptive dream of their Creator. Shalom will be realized, Zion will be incarnated, by the flow of God's Spirit in, through, and among us.

Though we seek God, we can never contain or control the mystery of "spirit." Our symbols and metaphors for spirit are fluid and non-confined. We speak of light and breath, wind and water, and know we still have not captured the awesome reality of God. The spiritual quest requires us to let go of what we are holding and receive what is holding us. A willingness to be soft and open, pliable and childlike, is essential to the process of spiritual formation.

Breath is an ancient symbol of spirit. It represents the invisible, life-giving presence of God that keeps our bodies and spirits alive. Breathing deeply can be a way of connecting with God. Breath can calm our bodies, center our minds, open our spirits to the Presence that is always with us. Praying with our breath can create a receptive space into which God's Spirit can flow. When we are filled with this inflowing of God's grace our hearts become expansive and compassionate. We become the people of God, the Community of Christ, as we create space for God to enter our deep places.

As you enter a new phase of your journey, trust this God who creates and calls, forms and transforms, heals and draws all into wholeness and joy. God is not far from us. God is in us and we are in God, and it shall be well with us.

Carolyn Brock,
[1]*Excerpts from* Called by a New Name

Going Deeper: The Trinity

The language of the "Trinity" was a formula of the "early church fathers"—men who studied, discussed, and wrote during the first five hundred years after Jesus' resurrection on how the Christian church should understand God. It was developed in the context of that day and the culture to explain an understanding of the relationship of God to humanity and the relationship between God the Father (parent), God the Son (Jesus Christ), and God the Holy Spirit.

Over time the meanings changed as language and contexts changed, while the Trinity transcended language and culture because of its very nature of divine mystery.

Rethinking and reinterpreting the Trinity as a way of understanding God for our day and time is crucial. It is especially important as a tool for reintroducing God to the postmodern world that accepts mystery and communicates through symbols.

Dale Luffman,
[2]*Excerpts from "An Account of God: A Trinitarian Reflection"*

The one eternal, living God is triune: one God in three persons. The God who meets people in the testimony of Israel is the same God who meets them in Jesus Christ and who dwells within creation as the Holy Spirit.

Icons of Christianity

Through the centuries, images have been used to help humanity express its understanding of the mysteries of the divine.

Elizabeth A. Johnson has reminded us that the specific Christian way of speaking about God is to speak of God in Trinitarian terms.[3] In an article published in *Theology Today*, titled "Trinity: To Let the Symbol Sing Again," Johnson described an icon of the Holy Trinity painted by a fifteenth-century Russian artist, Andrei Rublev. The painting of three strangers, sitting at a table is housed in the Trechikov Gallery. Reflecting on the icon, which represents Yahweh's (God's) visit to Abraham and Sarah, Johnson writes:

> *What catches the meditating eye most is the position of the three figures. They are arranged in a circle inclining toward one another but the circle is not closed. What the image suggests is that the mystery of God is not a self-contained or closed divine society but a communion in relationship. Moreover, its portrayal of figures evokes the idea that this divine communion is lovingly open to the world, seeking to nourish it.*
>
> *As you contemplate, you begin intuitively to grasp that you are invited into this circle. Indeed, by gazing, you are already a part of it. This is a description of a Trinitarian God capable of immense hospitality who calls the world to join the feast.*

What does this image of the Trinity say to you?

What does this image of the Trinity say to you?

What does this image of the yin-yang say to you?

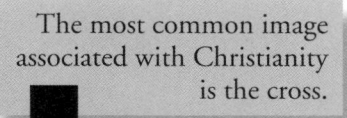

According to Jung Young Lee[4], the symbols of yin and yang can become important modes of understanding both the cosmos (creation) and humanity that are considered part of the Trinity. Lee also sees parallels between the Trinity as the "household of God" and an explanation of the yin and yang as a symbol using the characteristics of the family.

According to Lee, when the Trinity is understood in Western concepts it becomes difficult to distinguish between one and three. With the self at center it is impossible for one to be three and three to be one. However, when understood from the yin-yang perspective, three and one are not only interdependent but also inseparably related one to another as one in three and three in one.

The most common image associated with Christianity is the cross.

What does the image of the empty cross say to you?

Describing God

Historically, in context of the ancient, male-dominated world, and translated into English, God is described most often in scripture as male. However, God's attributes (even in scripture) go well beyond what might be identified with either gender. Describing God completely is beyond the capacity of the human experience. However, it is important to describe God —and to continually grow in that understanding.

Write down at least three ways you would describe God.

1.

2.

3.

What limitations do you find in your words and thoughts when describing God?

- Exodus 3:14
- Psalm 23
- Isaiah 40:28
- Revelation 1:8

God is the eternal creator, the source of love, life, and truth. God actively loves and cares for each person. All things that exist owe their being to God. God alone is worthy of worship.

Jesus Who?

Jesus has many names in the scriptures. Look up the following scriptures and write down the names given to Jesus. Next to each name, write down what you think this means. Share these with one other person older than you and note how their interpretation differs from yours.

- Matthew 2:2 (3:2 IV)
- Matthew 21:3 (21:2 IV)
- Mark 1:1
- Mark 6:3 (6:4 IV)
- Luke 2:11
- Luke 7:16
- John 1:1
- John 3:2
- John 6:53
- John 10:11
- John 14:6–12
- John 15:15

The most significant reference is that of "Christ," which means "savior." Christians believe that God became human, took on a human form, and came to live among us to demonstrate a higher standard of living. He was crucified and resurrected on the third day to provide those who believe salvation from sin. While it is good to study and grow in your understanding of who Jesus was, it takes faith to know who Jesus is.

Jesus is God. Jesus is called "Emmanuel" in scriptures that translated means "God with us." Jesus is part of the Trinity. While rational thinkers might dismiss this, understanding God as Jesus gives us a very personal relationship and connection to God. This is the God of the New Testament.

The Holy Spirit

Entire denominations have been formed based on different understandings of the third aspect of the Trinity, the Holy Spirit. The Holy Spirit is described in scripture as the comforter. The promise of receiving the Holy Spirit was made by the post-resurrection Jesus before he ascended into heaven.

If Jesus is "God with us," the Holy Spirit is God moving in us. The Holy Spirit is the presence of God in our lives that moves us to love, honor, and worship God, to know that God is, and to affirm that what we believe is real. While we can understand the majesty of God by looking at the sunset, and believe that Jesus Christ lived and died through the testimony of scripture, it is the Holy Spirit that causes us to know this is reality.

In the past century the Holy Spirit was described as a burning in your soul. In scripture it was described as fire or wind. What image of today's world would you use to describe or explain the Holy Spirit?

The Spirit is God and therefore knows and understands the things that only God knows and understands. It is through the Holy Spirit, which comes from God, that people can know and understand the wisdom of God.
—1 Corinthians 2:9–12 paraphrased

- Luke 12:12 (12:14 IV)
- Acts 2
- 1 Corinthians 2:9–12

Fruits of the Spirit

Galatians 5:22–23

What does scripture promise if people let the Holy Spirit dwell within and guide them?

Design a Symbol

Create a new symbol that represents your understanding of a triune God (the Trinity of God as Father (Parent), God as Son, God as Holy Spirit). It can either be entirely new or you can borrow elements or the entire symbol from contemporary culture. Write out how this works for you.

I Am with You Always—Pray!

Jesus often went to God for comforting, questioning, reflecting, and understanding. He taught the disciples that they too could pray.

Prayer is a powerful way to connect with God. Remember, there is no right or wrong way to pray. Prayer is just your way of talking to God and therefore can take on many forms.

- Pray for insight and guidance as you enter into the study of this resource.
- Praise the God of all, the beginning and end, the Creator.
- Thank God for your many blessings and opportunities.
- Pray for someone who is in need of physical or spiritual healing.
- Pray for the needs of others.
- Pray for peace and justice in the world.
- Pray by letting yourself just be with God. Breathe in, breathe out. Be aware that each breath is God breathing in you.
- Pray by singing the words of a song or hymn.
- Pray by talking to God about your concerns.
- Pray by sharing your joys with God.
- Pray by asking God questions—sometimes you may even need to argue with God to understand.
- Pray by reading or listening to prayers written by others.
- Pray in the name of Jesus Christ.

Take time right now to pray.

By Grace You Are Saved

The empty cross reminds people that Jesus lived as an example for them. Even though he died on a cross, he overcame death and rose again. This is called Resurrection (celebrated at Easter). The Community of Christ is founded on the life, death, resurrection, and continued presence of Jesus Christ in human lives. In Jesus' death and resurrection, people understand the grace of God and the promise of eternal life. In Jesus' continuing presence through the Holy Spirit, people learn how much they are loved.

Make your own cross to wear, display, or share. The simple shape can be made by tying or gluing together sticks, flat nails, craftsticks, pieces of wood, or wire.

Other options: needlepoint the shape, paint or draw it, create from beads or modeling clay.

By grace you have been saved through faith, and this is not your own doing; it is the gift of God—not the result of works, so that one might boast. For we are what God has made us, created for good works, which God prepared beforehand to be our way of life.—Ephesians 2:8–10 NRSV adapted

Session Objectives

- To understand the origin of scriptures used by the Community of Christ

- To learn how to study and explore the scriptures

Scriptures of the Church

IMAGE Reflection

2

13

Learning from the Scriptures

How can we let the witness of scripture more fully shape our lives? By actually reading it, listening to it, and applying it. Scripture, like vitamins, can enrich life, but only if we are willing to take it in. Try taking in scripture in three different but complimentary ways: **"looking at," "looking with,"** and **"walking with."**

Looking at . . .

Looking at scripture is making sense of the words on the page. This stage investigates the "who, what, where, why, and when" of the text and requires use of our intellect. Focus on what is being said and how it fits into the whole picture. The point is to let the passage speak on its own terms. This step opens the door to letting in the scripture.

Looking with . . .

Looking with scripture confronts us with the real and living God as understood by the author and permits that same God to touch our lives too. It requires our emotions, imaginations, and an openness to revelation. It allows us to see ourselves and our world in the light of the passage and raises questions that relate it to our own struggles: trust, doubt, hearing God's call, failure, turning away, fear, forgiveness. Here we move beyond viewing the text as an object under our control to admitting it into our lives and letting it be the means of God's gracious outreach to us.

Walking with . . .

The last step brings balance. Walking with is the process by which we invite scripture to influence our words and deeds. In the simple phrases of James, this stage is about "doing the word" (James 1:22). Here we search for concrete ways to let the text take up residence in us. Moved beyond understanding the words, beyond believing in them, we face the risky business of living for God's kingdom. Our response to scripture can form in us the image of the one we proclaim—Jesus Christ.

Engaging with scripture is not like solving a puzzle; we do not look at a passage, "figure it out," and leave it behind for something else. Rather, the text is meant to be taken with us in the ongoing journey of discipleship. None can predict what doors will open as God's people deliberately, prayerfully, and expectantly study the sacred Word.

Anthony Chvala-Smith, theologian-in-residence, and Charmaine Chvala-Smith, [5]adapted from "A Becoming Faith—Wondering on the Way"

Exegesis (ek´ se jē´ sis), which means "to pull out," is a systematic approach to seeking greater understanding of the scriptures on multiple levels. For a growing understanding of the scriptures, this study process must continue throughout a disciple's life-long journey with Christ.

Looking at . . .

Read James 1:22. What is the author saying? Use a commentary to investigate the "who, what, where, why, and when" of the text.

Looking with . . .

What was the author's experience with God that would lead him to write this? What if you were faced with a similar circumstance? How does this scripture apply to today?

But be doers of the word, and not merely hearers who deceive themselves. For if any are hearers of the word and not doers, they are like those who look at themselves in a mirror; for they look at themselves and, on going away, immediately forget what they were like. But those who look into the perfect law, the law of liberty, and persevere, being not hearers who forget but doers who act—they will be blessed in their doing.
—James 1:22–25 NRSV

Walking with...

What is your response to this scripture? Are you, in fact, doers of the word? How have you been blessed in your doing?

Look at the image on page 13. This montage represents various ways the guidance that comes from the word of God has been recorded throughout the years.

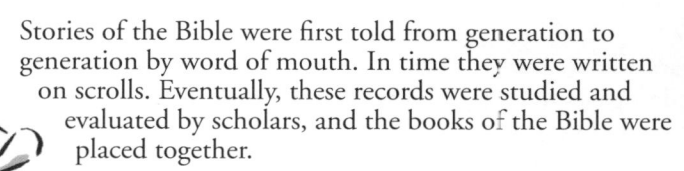

Stories of the Bible were first told from generation to generation by word of mouth. In time they were written on scrolls. Eventually, these records were studied and evaluated by scholars, and the books of the Bible were placed together.

Between the years 1947 and 1956 the Dead Sea Scrolls were discovered in caves along the northwest shore of the Dead Sea. They can be divided into two categories—biblical and non-biblical. Fragments of every book in the Hebrew canon (Old Testament) have been found among these findings except for the book of Esther. *(www.centuryone.com/25dssfacts.html)* Does this discovery make the words found in the Bible more or less sacred? Why or why not?

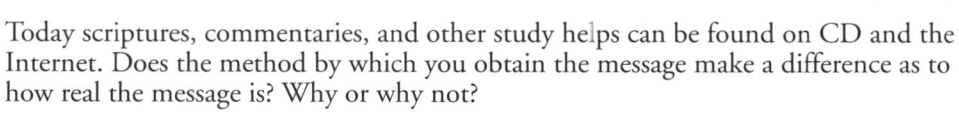

Today scriptures, commentaries, and other study helps can be found on CD and the Internet. Does the method by which you obtain the message make a difference as to how real the message is? Why or why not?

Messages about God's love can often be found on items like T-shirts, bumper stickers, and coffee mugs. How do you feel about sharing the message in these forms?

What's next? What form of communication do you think will be the next one used to convey God's message?

Community of Christ Scriptures

For centuries, the people of God have considered the sacred story important enough to share from one generation to the next, first in an oral tradition, then in writing. What we consider as scripture has a long and somewhat winding history. The message, however, has always focused on the activity of God in relationship to humankind. It is important to continue to expand the understanding of scripture as one seeks to develop a deeper relationship with God.

Read the opening pages of three different versions of the Bible. Many versions also contain introductions to each book. Skim through these as well. Compare the information found. From reading these pages, along with information you already understand, answer the questions.

- What is the Bible?

- What is the difference between the Old Testament (Hebrew Bible) and the New Testament?

- What differences did you find between the versions of the Bible you examined?

Read the introduction pages to the Book of Mormon and skim through the books. Then answer the question, "What is the Book of Mormon?"

The Community of Christ uses four "books" as sacred scripture (historically referred to as three): the Old Testament (Hebrew Bible), the New Testament, the Book of Mormon, and the Doctrine and Covenants.

What do these books of scripture have in common?

Read the introduction pages to the Doctrine and Covenants and skim through the sections. Then answer the question, "What is the Doctrine and Covenants?"

The Limits of Language

An important concept to understand about scripture is how limiting language is. Much of scripture is human expression of how God has done great things. Think about it. God has done great things in all of our lives, but how would you express it? You might write it down in words. Then you might revise it—especially as you grew older and reinterpreted it. What if you wanted to share it with someone who spoke only another language? You would have it translated. Then they could read it. But would they understand how you described the great thing God had done? What if a family member got a hold of it and told the same event in another way? In a similar way, this is what has happened to the sacred story. It explains why there are "translations," "versions," and "editions" of books that are considered sacred scripture.

The Community of Christ understands scripture to be a human story of what God has done (revelation). While the story is important, it is limited by our humanness—and even if it was written by ancient scholars—it still has the touch of human limitation.

> The process through which God reveals divine will and love is called revelation. God continues to reveal divine will today as in the past. God is revealed through scripture, the faith community, prayer, nature, and in human history.

Briefly describe one incredible thing God has done in your life.

Tell that event to someone else and then ask them to write it down—without your help.

Have them improve it in some way by rewriting it.

Ask someone else to read it and make improvements.

Translate it into another language (as possible).

Have someone else translate it back into the original language.

Compare the last writing with *your* original description. Any questions?

The Bible . . .

- is a book of books.
- took 1,600 years to write.
- was written by more than forty people including kings, fishermen, scholars, peasants, doctors, and tent-makers.
- was written from prisons, palaces, boats, and wilderness.
- was written on three continents: Asia, Africa, Europe.
- was written in three languages: Hebrew, Aramaic, and Greek.
- has been translated more than any other book.[6]

A Look Inside

Use indexes, concordances, and commentaries to find the following scripture stories. Write down the scripture references and discuss each one with your mentor and others.

Bible—Old Testament
- story of Moses leading the people out of Egypt
- story of Ruth and Naomi
- story of Esther
- story of Jonah

Bible—New Testament
Look through Matthew, Mark, Luke, and John (The Gospels). Jesus taught through stories (parables) and experiences. Identify parables Jesus told.

These examples were told by Jesus to relate to the people of that time. What can they mean to you today?

Book of Mormon
Read Alma 5:24–25, 27–28. When you are baptized, what promise are you making with God?

Doctrine and Covenants
Identify the sections of the Doctrine and Covenants that have been added since you were born.

Discuss how these sections are challenging today's church.

Scripture Survey

Using the following questions, survey members of the congregation (of various ages) about the scriptures used by the Community of Christ.

- What part of the sacred story is conveyed in each book of scripture?
- Which is your favorite book of scripture to use and why?
- What truths do the scriptures tell?

Record a summary of your findings here.

Session Objectives

- To describe the history of this faith community

- To identify places and events that created the Community of Christ

Community of Christ: Then and Now

IMAGE Reflection

3

Celebrate Our Story: Heritage as a Resource for the Future

Historical Foundations in a New Time

There is an extraordinary story of innovation, inspiration, courage, sacrifice, and adventure at the heart of our church. It begins with the search of a young boy to discover answers to questions that perplexed him in a time of religious fervor in his part of the world. Because he had a vision that gave him a sense of direction, Joseph Smith Jr. became the instrument for an amazing series of spiritual experiences and profound discoveries. Those attracted followers, and subsequently a church was formed under the direction of the boy, now grown to be a young man.

That church introduced what it believed to be a restoration of ancient truths, encapsulating them in an organizational form structured for the frontiers of nineteenth-century America. Misunderstood by neighbors, members of the church were driven from New York to Ohio to Missouri to Illinois. In each place, efforts were made to establish community founded on the word of God. Experimentation on economic matters, theological doctrines, social behaviors, and many other things led to both rapid growth and widespread opposition. The latter led ultimately to the assassination of Joseph Smith Jr., the young boy who first asked those questions and then led the church. In death, he became a martyr to the people who considered him a prophet.

It is not our purpose here to recite that story in any detail. Instead, we want to focus on elements of that story that are universal and that serve as a foundation for the contemporary church. The key question is how important historical concepts can inform us in a new era and how as a transformed people we can honor our past and at the same time become new people in Jesus Christ.

Honor the Past

Among the central and essential elements foundational both to the historical and the contemporary church are:

- ***The Centrality of Christ:*** Keep Jesus Christ at the center of your faith. Discover anew the ways his life and ministry can inform and inspire in a new era of human history.

- ***Community:*** Create new models of community that embrace the call of Jesus Christ to love one another and live together in peace.

- ***Pluralism:*** Create diverse pathways to faith that will breathe life and freedom into the reflection on God's word.

- ***Zion:*** Engage in the structures of this world through creative and loving service that embraces the totality of God's creation.

- ***All Are Called:*** Affirm the worth of all people, young and old, ordained and unordained, male and female, of every race and hue. Make sure each one finds their rightful place among the children of God.

- ***Discovering God's Spirit:*** Seek the Spirit in the many places where it can be found by sharing the prophetic task as visionaries and mystics and explorers, and by being receptive to where God is leading you, even into new frontiers.

We celebrate the story of our history because it sets the framework in which we come to understand our life together as God's people. It provides for us real life examples of discipleship and service.

Today it is our time to continue the story, building on the traditions and experiences of the past, but called by God into a new time in human history. It is a new day and God calls us forth once again to be a community of joy, hope, love, and peace.

[7]*Adapted from W. Grant McMurray, president, Community of Christ*

Look at the picture on page 19. What can be gained by bridging together the church's past, present, and future?

Talk to an adult who knows about the history of your family. How has your family's past affected where you are today?

What major changes do you observe happening in the world today?

How might these changes affect the culture and ministry of the church?

What do you believe the church is being called to do in this day and time?

Focusing on the essential elements to the historical and contemporary church as laid out by President McMurray, how can you honor the past in your journey of discipleship?

- The Centrality of Christ

- Zion

- Community

- All Are Called

- Pluralism

- Discovering God's Spirit

The First Christians

When Jesus walked the earth, he gathered many followers around him. As he taught them, ate with them, and shared his life with them, many chose to follow and learn the things he taught. Jesus reached out to many: healing, teaching, loving. He taught his followers and called his disciples to do what he had done.

The early Christian church developed as his disciples shared the message of Jesus, who they called the Christ. They invited others to join and share in community with them and their risen Lord. As the church grew, different and diverse beliefs were often expressed. In response to the leading of the Holy Spirit, a collection of beliefs and practices emerged to guide the lives of the disciples. These included "apostolic" teaching, the church giving witness to what the apostles had taught, as well as agreed-on understandings of the gospel or "rules of faith." These were understood through the reading of the Hebrew Bible (Old Testament) and the emergence of the New Testament scriptures.

Through the years, the church grew and was led by the Holy Spirit in defining its faith so that the disciples could effectively witness in their changing circumstances. Over time, clarification was given to many important doctrines such as the Trinity, the divinity and humanity of Christ, and understandings of the sacraments.

Sometimes conflicts emerged as the church sought to understand the faith that it was called to share with the world. In such moments faithful leaders, such as Athanasius, Augustine, and Martin Luther, came forward and assisted the church in its growing understanding of the gospel.

If you had lived when Jesus was on earth, would you have been one of his followers? Why or why not?

What draws you to or away from the church today?

Pray for Understanding

In the early 1800s in the United States, many leaders of different beliefs would hold meetings and revivals preaching different ways of following Jesus. A young teen named Joseph Smith Jr. was especially confused. One day while reading, Smith read from James 1:5. He decided to ask God for help. While seeking God in the solitude of the woods near his home, young Joseph encountered the Divine. The experience of Joseph Smith Jr. that day in the woods was the seeds of beginning for a new faith community.

What concerns do you need to talk to God about?

Scripture Study

If any of you is lacking in wisdom, ask God, who gives to all generously and ungrudgingly, and it will be given you.
—James 1:5 NRSV

Go to a place where you connect with God. Spend time in prayer, talking with God about your concerns and questions.

Organization of the Church

On April 6, 1830, Joseph Smith Jr. and a small group of family and friends officially organized the church in the state of New York.

Kirtland, Ohio

As the United States expanded westward, the small church group moved west to Kirtland, Ohio. The church community continued to grow. There the church built a temple, established a school, and practiced the belief of sharing all things in common so there would be no poor. The hymn, "The Spirit of God Like a Fire Is Burning" was sung at the dedication of the Kirtland temple.

The Church in Missouri

In 1838, the church began a new community in Jackson County, Missouri. But as church members gathered to the area, they struggled with how to form a religious community and at the same time be a community with neighbors of different beliefs. This struggle went both ways, and soon the church moved out of Jackson County to Caldwell County, Missouri. In this county, created specifically for them, a community of over 5,000 people gathered.

Find Palmyra, New York, and Kirtland, Ohio, on a United States map. Look up "The Spirit of God Like a Fire Is Burning" (*Hymns of the Saints* 33). Read or sing the words of the song. Imagine yourself joyfully singing along with others at the temple dedication.

Find Jackson County, Missouri; Nauvoo, Illinois; and Independence, Missouri. How far are these locations from where you live?

Nauvoo, Illinois

The church people moved from Missouri across the Mississippi River. There they cleared out swamp land to create a city called Nauvoo. People came from all over the world to live in Nauvoo. Soon this church community grew to be almost the size of the city of Chicago at that time. In Nauvoo people could find schools—including a university—stores, and the houses of church leaders. The town had its own militia and Joseph Smith Jr. served as mayor.

While in Nauvoo, anger against the church became stronger. Joseph Smith Jr. and other leaders were imprisoned several times. During one of those times, Joseph Smith Jr. was killed. Church members struggled about what to do next. Many decided to follow Brigham Young to Utah, while others went different ways. Joseph's wife, Emma, stayed with her children in Nauvoo.

Several years later, a newly reorganized group invited Joseph Smith III to lead them, and on April 6, 1860, the Reorganized Church of Jesus Christ of Latter Day Saints was organized at Amboy, Illinois. Joseph Smith III was president of the church for fifty-four years. During those years, the church membership grew to more than seventy thousand people.

Headquarters in Independence, Missouri

The church eventually moved back to Independence, Missouri, where many years earlier Joseph Smith Jr. had dedicated a temple site. The headquarters of the church remains there today where the Auditorium and Temple serve the community and the church as symbols of the church's mission to create communities of joy, hope, love, and peace.

Talk with people who have lived in your area for a long time. When and how did the Community of Christ come to your community?

Community of Christ Mission Statement

"We proclaim Jesus Christ and promote communities of joy, hope, love, and peace."

What does it mean to proclaim Jesus Christ in the world today?

Describe your vision of what communities of joy, hope, love, and peace look like.

On a world map, mark the places where the Community of Christ has presence today.

Community of Christ

Since the reorganization of the church, membership has grown to over 250,000 members worldwide. The current church president is W. Grant McMurray. On April 6, 2001, the church officially changed the name to Community of Christ—a name that more globally represents the church's mission.

Misunderstandings

Many of the problems in Community of Christ history arose because people in the community did not understand the goals and beliefs of the church members. What are misunderstandings people in your community might have about the Community of Christ today? How do these misunderstandings make you feel? What can you do to help others understand the mission of Community of Christ?

Research three of these countries to understand more about your brothers and sisters in the Community of Christ.

Countries where the Community of Christ has presence (as of April 2002).

American Samoa
Argentine Republic
Kingdom of Belgium
Kingdom of Denmark
Kingdom of Spain
Kingdom of Sweden
Republic of Bulgaria
Republic of Colombia
Republic of Estonia
Union of Myanmar
Aruba
Chile
France
Guatemala
Hungary
Russia
Ukraine
Zimbabwe
Bolivia
South Africa
Kingdom of Nepal
Sri Lanka
Malawi
El Salvador
Jamaica
Côte d' Ivoire
Zambia
Democratic Republic of the Congo
Dominican Republic
Kenya
Liberia
China
Honduras
New Caledonia
Haiti
Fiji
Philippines
India
Nigeria
Peru
Brazil
Mexico
Republic of Korea
Japan
Grand Cayman
Germany
New Zealand
Norway
Netherlands
French Polynesia
Australia
United Kingdom
Canada
United States

Session Objectives

- To identify the eight sacraments practiced by the Community of Christ

- To learn the basic purpose for each sacrament

- To learn how individuals participate in each sacrament

Church Sacraments

IMAGE Reflection

4

25

Being in Touch with God—the Sacraments

[8]Excerpts taken from Seekers and Disciples

God is encountered through the sacraments of the church, which touch life at important times and places. Sacraments bring together the influence of the Holy Spirit, the example of the life of Jesus Christ, and one's personal commitment of faith. Through the sacraments one discovers the presence of God everywhere and that all life is potentially sacred. These encounters point to God's loving desire to bring all humans to peace, wholeness, and right relationships with one another and the Divine. That is what is meant by *salvation*.

In the Community of Christ there are eight sacraments, which are celebrated in worship experiences at appropriate times.

Blessing of Children—*honoring the children of God*

Baptism—*covenanting with God and one another*

Confirmation—*receiving the strength for discipleship*

Communion—*remembering Christ, commitment, and community*

Ordination—*a calling to serve people*

Laying On of Hands—*healing of spirit and body*

Marriage—*blessing a life-long partnership*

Evangelist's Blessing—*spiritual guidance in the disciple's path*

God Is with Us:
Testimonies of Pat Long and Jim Long from Toronto, Canada

Pat

I approach the sacraments with what might be called "a spiritual excitement." While each of these encounters has special meaning to me, I am always deeply touched by Communion. Each month I approach this sacramental service with hope as well as remembrance and renewal. I am blessed to be able to share the bread and wine with a friend with whom I was baptized and confirmed. We shared our first Communion together. Often during the service, I remember the joy we felt as little girls so happy to be able to receive the bread and wine with our equally happy parents.

I tend to equate the Communion table to the table around which I sat as the second youngest of twelve children. I have a warm feeling as I recall good memories of active conversations and quiet moments when you could just sit unnoticed and feel the love. I feel that same warmth and love when I come to the table the Lord has symbolically prepared for me. I remember the sacrifice Christ made for me. As I take the bread I begin to share a special time with the Spirit of Christ that is just for me. With eyes closed I sense that Jesus and I are together. I share with him my hope that the bread will strengthen me for the things he has for me to do. When I receive the wine, I pray the Holy Spirit will flow through me so that I might see others as Jesus would see them. After experiencing the Communion I feel pure and whole and eager to follow the person by whose name I am called. I won't miss the Communion if I can possibly help it.

Jim

In my early teens I left the church in which I had been raised. The sacraments had not been especially meaningful for me. Later, as a young adult, I realized that for those participating in the Community of Christ, the sacraments were very meaningful. I was baptized. When I was confirmed my whole body tingled. I now see that was the moment when I began a new relationship with the Lord. I had invited Jesus Christ into my life, and he came.

I now serve the church as an evangelist. As I have shared in sacramental experiences with many people over the years, I have witnessed the testimony of God's loving presence in their lives. This is especially true as I am present to share in prayer for those who are sick. They receive peace, comfort, and healing. This ministry of healing is experienced for many different circumstances. I recall having the elders place their hands on my head and pray for me just before I left home for an important assignment. I was so concerned about what I needed to do that I became ill. I was afraid my concerns would affect my judgment. As I began my assignment there were setbacks that seemed to threaten success. In each case, however, I felt the spirit of that prayer freeing me to use all my skills and knowledge. The outcome of that trip and my assignment was very positive. I have seen this same healing experience with others for whom I have prayed.

Time after time the sacraments have convinced me that God is with us all.

Which of the sacraments have you observed?

Which of the sacraments have you participated in and what did you gain from those experiences?

Ask people in the congregation to share their testimonies of what the sacraments mean to them.

> Look especially to the sacraments to enrich the spiritual life of the body. Seek for greater understanding of my purposes in these sacred rites and prepare to receive a renewed confirmation of the presence of my Spirit in your experiences of worship.
> —Doctrine and Covenants 158:11c

Blessing of Children

- Doctrine and Covenants 17:19
- Matthew 19:13–15
- Mark 10:13–16
- Luke 18:15–17
- III Nephi 8:12–13, 23–24

This sacrament is available to any who ask. A child up to the age of baptism (eight years old) can be blessed. Parents choose to bring their child to two elders for a blessing. This is usually done as part of a worship service in the congregation. A baby is usually handed to one elder who cradles the child securely. A young child may sit in a chair or on a parent's lap. Parents, siblings, or other family members gather around. The other elder places hands on the child and offers a prayer asking God to bless the child and the family. Joint responsibility is placed on the natural family and the congregational family.

Interview families who have brought their children to the elders to be blessed. Why did they choose to do so, and what was the experience like for them?

Baptism is a promise between an individual and God. It is a personal decision. Through baptism a person promises to try to live each day as a disciple of Christ. Following the example of Jesus, people (ages eight and older) in the Community of Christ are baptized by immersion by a priest or elder. Emerging from the water symbolizes washing away "the old" and starting new with Christ.

Baptism

- Doctrine and Covenants 17:21
- Moroni 6:1–5
- Matthew 3:11–17
- Mark 1:1–11
- Luke 3:21–22
- Romans 6:1–11
- 1 Corinthians 12:12–13

Seeking baptism?

Who would you like to baptize and confirm you?

As you seek to understand and enrich your relationship with Christ, what does baptism and confirmation mean for you?

Confirmation

- Doctrine and Covenants 17:8c
- II Nephi 13:12–16
- Moroni 2:1–3
- Mark 1:8
- John 14:15–20
- Acts 8:15–17

This church believes in a two-part baptism. Baptism in water is the first part of the experience. Confirmation is the second. The candidate sits in a chair with an elder standing on either side. The elders lay their hands on the person's head and one of them offers the confirmation prayer, asking for the gift of the Holy Spirit in the life of the new member. The Holy Spirit is represented symbolically as a flame, dove, or comforter.

Communion

- Doctrine and Covenants 17:22a–23b
- Luke 22:7–20
- III Nephi 8:28–41
- Moroni 4:1–4, 5:1–3

The sacrament of Communion is for people who have made a covenant with God. Participate in Communion service. Prior to going, spend time in prayer and preparation. Record thoughts from the experience.

It is expedient that the church meet together often to partake of bread and wine in remembrance of the Lord Jesus; and the elder or priest shall administer it; and after this manner shall he [or she] administer it.
—Doctrine and Covenants 17:22a–b

Music

Search hymnals for songs about the sacraments.

Ordination

- Doctrine and Covenants 17:12a–b
- Moroni 3:1–3
- Luke 10:1–17
- 1 Corinthians 12:27–31
- Exodus 28:1–5
- 1 Peter 2:4–5
- Ephesians 4:11–13

Learn more about priesthood in the next session.

Priesthood members are called of God to special service. Aaronic members are deacons, priests, and teachers. Melchisedec members include elders, high priests, seventy, evangelists, bishops, apostles, and the prophet. The ordinand prepares with prayer and study in special classes. The ordination takes place in the congregation. Two priesthood members with authority ordain the candidate, naming the office of calling. Priesthood are servant ministers.

Laying On of Hands
[Administration]

- Doctrine and Covenants 42:12d
- Luke 4:38–40
- James 5:14–17

Visit with people who have participated in the laying on of hands—both elders and individuals who have asked for administration.

Anyone who has a need can ask for prayer from the elders. This applies to members and friends. The scripture base for this sacrament can be found in James 5:14. The elders stand on either side of the person. One elder puts a drop of consecrated oil on the person's head and asks for the presence of the Holy Spirit. Both elders lay their hands gently on the head of the person, and the second elder offers a special prayer. Blessings from administration come in many forms.

Marriage

- Doctrine and Covenants 111:2a
- Hebrew 13:4

Marriage is the beginning of a new family as two people covenant for life. Each individual is willing to share, care, love, trust, help, and understand in new ways. This church holds vows of marriage sacred.

Priests or elders may perform a wedding service. Premarital discussions are recommended.

A vow before God is a serious commitment. What characteristics would you like to have in a life partner?

Studying in a group?

- Act out the sacraments as each one is described.

- Invite members from the congregation to explain each sacrament.

- Visit parts of the church where the sacraments take place. Investigate the baptismal font, the view from a chair on the platform, and see where the Communion materials are kept and prepared.

- Help prepare the bread and juice for a Communion service. If possible, bake the bread to be used.

Evangelist's Blessing

- Doctrine and Covenants 125:3b
- 2 Timothy 4:1–5

Speak to an evangelist about getting a blessing. What questions are you pondering at this time?

People can ask God to bless and guide them throughout their lives. This special ministry is available to members and friends of the church. The one seeking the blessing must have faith in God, understand what it means to make a covenant, and be willing to accept the ministry of the evangelist. The evangelist helps the person prepare for the blessing. A copy of the blessing is made for the person to read again for strength and guidance.

Session Objectives

- To renew your spirit
- To discover ways you can serve the Lord
- To learn about the specific type of ministry called priesthood

Called to Serve the Lord

IMAGE Reflection

5

Gifts of All Create the Body

There are different kinds of gifts, but the same Spirit. There are different kinds of service, but the same Lord. There are different kinds of working, but the same God works all of them.

Now to each one the manifestation of the Spirit is given for the common good. To one there is given through the Spirit the message of wisdom, to another the message of knowledge by means of the same Spirit, to another faith by the same Spirit, to another gifts of healing by that one Spirit, to another miraculous powers, to another prophecy, to another distinguishing between spirits, to another speaking in different kinds of languages, and to still another the interpretation of languages. All these are the work of one and the same Spirit, as God determines.

The body is a unit, though it is made up of many parts; and though all its parts are many, they form one body. So it is with Christ. For we were all baptized by one Spirit into one body—whether Jews or Greeks, servant or free—and we were all given the one Spirit to drink.

Now the body is not made up of one part but of many. If the foot should say, "Because I am not a hand, I do not belong to the body," it would not for that reason cease to be part of the body. And if the ear should say, "Because I am not an eye, I do not belong to the body," it would not for that reason cease to be part of the body. If the whole body were an eye, where would the sense of hearing be? If the whole body were an ear, where would the sense of smell be? But in fact God has arranged the parts in the body, every one of them. If they were all one part, where would the body be? As it is there are many parts, but one body.

The eye cannot say to the hand, "I don't need you!" And the head cannot say to the feet, "I don't need you!" On the contrary, those parts of the body that seem to be weaker are indispensable, and the parts that we think are less honorable we treat with special honor. And the parts that are unpresentable are treated with special modesty, while our presentable parts need no special treatment. But God has combined the members of the body and has given greater honor to the parts that lacked it, so that there should be no division in the body, but that its parts should have equal concern for one another. If one part suffers, every part suffers with it; if one part is honored, every part rejoices with it.

Now you are the body of Christ, and each one of you is a part of it. And in the church God has appointed first of all apostles, second prophets, third teachers, then workers of miracles, also those having gifts of healing, those able to help others, those with gifts of administration, and those speaking in different languages.

—*1 Corinthians 12:1–28 NIV adapted* [9]

What does 1 Corinthians 12:1–28 say about your gifts and talents?

If God has given each person gifts important to the body of Christ, what gifts can you identify in people at church?

How do the many gifts of your congregation come together to create a ministry of wholeness?

Write a poem, rap, or song that interprets 1 Corinthians 12:1–28 and the value of all people in God's eyes.

A Centering Prayer

A centering prayer, such as the one described below, may help to cultivate your personal relationship with the One who loves and calls.

This time of meditation requires you to step back from the pressures and expectations of daily living, to let go, and "just be" with God.

Sit in a chair, on a pillow, or on the floor, but don't lie down. Place your hands in your lap with palms upward as if you are holding or receiving something.

For the next few minutes you will think or speak a word, the same word, over and over—almost as if you are slowly breathing it. This phrase is called a mantra. Many phrases or words can be used, but to start use the phrase, "just be."

Once in position, close your eyes and begin. Breathe deep and slow. Breathe in, "just be." Breathe out, "just be." Don't worry about what you are suppose to feel or think. **Just be!** If your mind starts to wander, refocus on your mantra: breathe in, "just be." Breathe out, "just be."

Continue your meditation for ten minutes. *(Setting a timer before you start will free your mind from the time.)* You will be amazed at how quickly the time passes.

Try the method of a centering prayer.
How did you feel at the end of the experience?

Reflection

After you have taken the time to "just be" with God, use art or words to let your soul respond to the statement "God is calling me . . ."

All Are Called

God calls all people to share in the ministry of the church. Look up the scriptures listed below. How did the people described in the scriptures react to their calling? What lessons can be learned from each one?

Women
- mother and sister of Moses (Exodus 2:1–10)
- Mary, Jesus' mother (Luke 2:1–7)
- woman at the well (John 4:6–10, 25–30 [8–12, 27–32 IV])
- Lydia (Acts 16:13–15)

Men
- Jonah (Jonah 3:1–5, 10)
- Peter (Matthew 16:16–18 [17–19 IV])
- Saul (Acts 9:10–19)
- Alma (Mosiah 9:38–45)

Children/Youth
- Samuel (1 Samuel 3:1–10)
- Jehoash (2 Kings 11:12, 12:1–2)
- child who shared loaves and fishes (John 6:5–11)
- Abish, maid of King Lamoni's queen (Alma 12:148–180)

Ministry Needs

Ask other youth, children, and adults to share in this activity. If at all possible, include people who are friends, members, deacons, teachers, priests, elders, and evangelists. Provide each person with signs that explain the priesthood they are representing. These should include the priesthood offices as well as members and friends. You may need multiples of some of the signs, especially member. Write the ministry needs on slips of paper, then place them in a basket.

visit someone who is sick
a child's pet died
share a testimony
give a ride to church
teach a song
preach a sermon
perform a marriage
take up offering
ordain someone as a priest
give an evangelist's blessing
help with tithing
teach a youth class
be a youth leader
help with potluck
help on church work day
baptize a new member
say a prayer

Ask everyone to stand around the room, leaving the center open. Let candidates draw slips of paper from the basket one at a time. When the ministry need is read, the candidates should bring the people who can fulfill this need into the center. Many ministries can be performed by more than one priesthood member (for instance, preaching, teaching, baptizing, or serving the Lord's Supper). If a member or friend can also meet that need, they would be brought into the center. Everyone should return to the outside of the room before the next slip of paper is drawn and read. Help young children realize that they, too, can meet many of the ministry needs.

This is a wonderful activity for the whole congregation.

Go to a light source such as a lamp or a light switch. Turn the light on and off a few times. The light of God is similar to these sources. The power is always there, always a part of you, it is just waiting to be shared with others (Matthew 5:14–16).

You Have the Power to Share the Light

Describe an experience in which you felt the Spirit prompting you to share the light of God with others.

Ask priesthood and members to share their testimonies of calling and service.

Priesthood Scripture Study

All Members
    Doctrine and Covenants 17:18–19, 1 Corinthians 12
Apostles
    Doctrine and Covenants 104:12, Matthew 10:2
Bishops
    Doctrine and Covenants 104:8, 1 Timothy 3:1–7
Deacons
    Doctrine and Covenants 17:11d–f, 1 Timothy 3:8–11
Elders
    Doctrine and Covenants 17:8–9, 1 Timothy 5:17
Evangelists
    Ephesians 4:11, Acts 21:8, 2 Timothy 4:5
High Priests
    Doctrine and Covenants 104:5, Hebrews 8:3
Priests
    Doctrine and Covenants 17:10, Genesis 14:18
Prophet/President
    Doctrine and Covenants 104:42, Ephesians 4:11–13
Seventies
    Doctrine and Covenants 17:8, 104:13
Teachers
    Doctrine and Covenants 17:11, Ephesians 4:11–13

Priesthood

There are specific "functions" or ministries in the church that are also called offices of the priesthood. The Community of Christ recognizes many priesthood offices. When people are called to be priesthood members, they are then ordained, which is a sacrament of the Community of Christ. Ordination is a calling to serve in a special way, yet everyone who chooses to be a disciple of Jesus is called to share in the gifts they have. The ministries of priesthood are given through Christ to equip the church for ministry!

All Members are called to serve and minister according to the gifts they have been given.

Apostles travel throughout the world, share testimonies of Jesus Christ, are high priests, and oversee large areas of the church.

> I say to you now, as I have said in the past, that all are called according to the gifts which have been given them. This applies to priesthood as well as to any other aspects of the work.—Doctrine and Covenants 156:9b

Bishops gather and use church offerings, use money wisely for the church, and teach about stewardship.

Deacons encourage attendance, care for church property, help with physical needs, and teach members to be good stewards.

Elders assist with administrations, ordain other priesthood members, baptize and confirm new members, and are leaders of congregations.

Evangelists give special blessings, comfort people, visit different congregations, teach, and preach.

High Priests teach and preach, have authority to serve in any other office, and may serve in charge of mission centers.

Priests bring ministry to families, perform marriages, baptize, and serve the Lord's Supper.

Prophet/President is the leader of the church, and brings messages from God to people.

Seventies serve as missionaries, are elders, invite others to join God's family, and preach.

Teachers are peacemakers, counsel with people, see that the church meets often, and reconcile differences.

A Ministry Tool List Based on Giftedness

> Identify the gifts that describe you. List ways you can use these gifts for ministry.

Gift of Helping
- ○ willingness
- ○ patience
- ○ enthusiasm
- ○ follows directions

Gift of Encouraging
- ○ likes to telephone others
- ○ likes to e-mail or chat
- ○ supportive
- ○ sees good in others

Gift of Giving
- ○ willing to share
- ○ can save money
- ○ has possessions
- ○ wants to make a difference

Gift of Teaching
- ○ can explain things
- ○ enjoys people
- ○ likes to share knowledge
- ○ sees possibilities

Gift of Pastoring
- ○ good listener
- ○ slow to judge
- ○ accepts all people
- ○ sees other's strengths

Gift of Mercy
- ○ cares for sick
- ○ mediator
- ○ service oriented
- ○ aware of other's needs

Gift of Hospitality
- ○ likes to host
- ○ gracious
- ○ concern for people
- ○ inviting

Gift of Leading
- ○ organizer
- ○ confidence
- ○ decision maker
- ○ carries things through

Gift of Evangelism
- ○ testimony of Christ
- ○ seeks to live witness
- ○ lives in community
- ○ stands for beliefs

Gift of Faith
- ○ prays for others
- ○ risks with God
- ○ willing to believe
- ○ hope and understanding

Gift of Friendship
- ○ supportive
- ○ trusting
- ○ team player
- ○ unconditional love

Gift of Joy
- ○ friendly
- ○ lots of energy
- ○ positive
- ○ loves to laugh

Session Objectives

- To learn that tithing is money given generously as a response to the generous gifts God gives

- To understand that a disciple is a committed member who makes a generous response in congregational life and to the world

- To discuss generous responses to God's gifts of love and grace

A Disciple's Generous Response

IMAGE Reflection

6

A Disciple's Generous Response [10]

Church leaders and members have, over many years, been exploring God's scriptural encouragement to view stewardship of our money in light of God's grace and love as demonstrated in the life of Jesus Christ.

Tithing is deeply rooted in the scriptures and affirms God's generous gifts of grace and love. The spirit of generosity is not about mathematical formulas but about thankfulness. Therefore, a disciple's generous response asks, "How much can I hope to give?" rather than "How much should I give?"

> Let whoever is of a generous heart bring the LORD's offering.
> —Exodus 35:5 NRSV

Tithing is . . .

- Tithing is money shared generously as a response to the generous gifts God gives.

- A disciple's tithing response expresses love of God, neighbor, creation, and self.

- The principle of tithing is a response of thanksgiving and is contributed first.

Mission Tithes—a disciple's response (the giving of money) to world and local missions of the church.

For example
- Local congregational ministries
- World Church ministries
- Oblation/ministry for the poor
- World Hunger Fund
- Camping ministries
- Other designated projects

> Let the truths of my gospel be proclaimed as widely and as far as the dedication of the Saints, especially through the exercise of their temporal stewardship, will allow.—Doctrine and Covenants 153:9a

Community Tithes—a disciple's response (giving of money) to church-affiliated organizations and other charitable nonprofit organizations that are *"in the forefront . . . recognizing the worth of persons and are committed to bringing the ministry of my Son to bear on their lives"* (Doctrine and Covenants 151:9).

For example:
- Graceland University
- Outreach International
- Restoration Trail Foundation
- Saints Care (Australia)
- The Groves Retirement Community
- World Accord (Canada)
- Other charitable nonprofit organizations

Saving is . . .

- The principle of saving is an expression of hope for the future. Disciples save in order to create a better tomorrow for themselves, their families, the church, and the world.

For example
- Reserves for unexpected needs
- Retirement funds
- College funds
- Estates for family and church

> For which of you, intending to build a tower, does not first sit down and estimate the cost, to see whether he has enough to complete it?
> —Luke 14:28 NRSV

Responsible Spending is . . .

Responsible spending is a disciple's use of their remaining income for supporting family, personal needs, and developing talents and interests. For example
- Housing
- Health care
- Transportation
- Food
- Clothing
- Recreation
- Personal development

> It is incumbent upon the Saints . . . to be in the world but not of it, living and acting honestly and honorably before God and in the sight of all [people], using the things of this world in the manner designed of God, that the places where they occupy may shine as Zion.
> —Doctrine and Covenants 128:8b–c

Where does the money you spend come from?

How do you spend most of the money you receive?

Who pays for your food, shelter, clothes, and school supplies?

When was the last time you gave money to the church or to a "good cause"?

Do you have a savings account?

If someone gave you $3,000 to spend any way you want, how would you spend it and how long do you think it would take you to do so?

What does responsible giving, saving, and spending have to do with being a disciple of Christ?

Widow's Mite: Mark 12:41–44

Read the story of the widow's offering. What did Jesus say about her giving? How does that relate to the way you give and spend?

To respond as a generous disciple means making choices about how you live so that you have the capacity to continue to increase your generosity.

Rich Young Ruler: Mark 10:17–31

What choices are you ready to make?

In a world where credit cards are given to college students like candy, credit and debt have become an accepted way of life. Free and easy money—that's what it feels like—but the responsibility still belongs to the card holder. If you charge it, *you* owe it! To use credit cards is to borrow against your future.

Do you have offering envelopes? If not, ask your pastor to get them for you.

Give Generously

What does a generous response look like? Take a loaf of bread, a pie, or a cake, and cut it in ten sections. Remove one piece to represent the giving of one tenth. Look again. If you were sharing with a stranger, how much would you be willing to give? If you were sharing with a friend, how much would you give? If you were sharing with someone who hadn't eaten in three days, how much would you give? If Jesus were sitting at your table, how much would you give?

Do the sidebar activity. How did you respond in each case? Was it always the same? Why or why not?

Blessings from 1 to 10

Even in the hardest of times, through the love and grace of God, we are blessed. List ten blessings that fill your life each day.

1
2
3
4
5
6
7
8
9
10

Sharing because God Loves You

Sharing does not always happen with money and things. God also calls us to share our love, our time, our talents, our knowledge, and our witness. What can you share?

Stewardship is the response of my people to the ministry of my Son and is required alike of all those who seek to build the kingdom.
—Doctrine and Covenants 147:5a

You Did It Also to Me

For I was hungry and you gave me food, I was thirsty and you gave me something to drink, I was a stranger and you welcomed me, I was naked and you gave me clothing, I was sick and you took care of me, I was in prison and you visited me.

. . . Lord, when was it that we saw you hungry and gave you food, or thirsty and gave you something to drink? And when was it that we saw you a stranger and welcomed you, or naked and gave you clothing? And when was it that we saw you sick or in prison and visited you?

. . . Truly I tell you, just as you did it to one of the least of these who are members of my family, you did it to me.—Matthew 25:35–40 NRSV

How can you help the hungry in your community?

How can you help the homeless, the poor, the needy?

How can you help the sick or imprisoned who need your ministry?

Is there someone who needs your understanding? your friendship? your unconditional love? How will you help them?

God loves a cheerful giver.
—2 Corinthians 9:7 NRSV

Enough for All

Arrange to share this object lesson on the concept of generous giving as a children's moment in a worship or for children's class.

Music Idea
"Lord, I Give You,"
NS 32

Use one single sheet of paper to illustrate the following.

"God has blessed me in many ways. Each corner on this piece of paper represents a blessing. It has four corners. *(Count them aloud.)* We are called to share generously with others. *(Tear a square off one corner of the paper and give it to a student.)* When I shared, what happened? What does my friend have? *(Count corners of friend's square.)* Do I have less because I shared? *(Count the corners of your paper—now five. Continue until everyone has a piece of the paper.)* When you give generously in response to God's blessings, you also receive." Close with prayer, thanking God for all blessings.

Financial Management

To be able to generously give financially, a disciple must also be a wise manager of their money.

- Talk with your parents (or other responsible adult) about what expenses are required to run a family household in your community.

- Look ahead to plans for your future. Do they include college or skill training? If so, how will you pay for it? If you have not done so already, establish a savings account in your name.

- Copy the monthly record sheet (see page 42) and use to record how you give and spend money.

RECORD OF INCOME RECEIVED

Date:	$ Amount:	Date:	$ Amount:
From:		From:	
Date:	$ Amount:	Date:	$ Amount:
From:		From:	
Date:	$ Amount:	Date:	$ Amount:
From:		From:	
Date:	$ Amount:	Date:	$ Amount:
From:		From:	

TITHING SHARED

Date:	$ Amount:
To:	
Date:	$ Amount:
To:	
Date:	$ Amount:
To:	
Date:	$ Amount:
To:	

MONEY SAVED

Date:	$ Amount:
How:	
Date:	$ Amount:
How:	
Date:	$ Amount:
How:	
Date:	$ Amount:
How:	

Record of Responsible Spending

Month:

Year:

Name:

Date	Description of Expenditures	$ Amount

Session Objectives

- To see the individual as part of many larger communities, including the Community of Christ

- To learn to value the worth of all people

- To accept the call as a disciple of Christ to promote communities of peace and justice

Discipleship in Community

IMAGE Reflection

7

Oh, the Joy! Reflections on Baseball and Discipleship

When I was ten, I was captured by baseball. I couldn't read enough biographies or novels about "The Game," listen to enough broadcasts on the radio, memorize enough major league line-ups, collect enough baseball cards, or learn enough statistics. But mostly, I couldn't play enough!

Through college years I played on organized teams and forever after at camps, reunions, and in a softball league in Nairobi, Kenya, East Africa—whenever opportunity permitted. Even in my first years in the Council of Twelve I kept a glove and ball in the trunk so that when I made it to the real field of dreams on a ministry trip through eastern Iowa, I was ready. I'm *still* ready!

I'm quite happy to prove why baseball is the perfect game, better than all others. . . but I would digress if I headed in that direction.

Some would say that the ultimate goal of baseball is to make it to "the show," to the major leagues. And they would be right . . . in part. But the reason for the thousands of swings of the bat and the hundreds of hours of practice; the reason for fielding all those grounders, running all those miles after fly balls, and considering yourself successful if you get on base three times out of ten, is not just to make the majors. Only a small fraction do that. The reason for doing all those things is finally about the pure joy of it all.

It's about discovering dimensions of yourself that you didn't realize before. It's about blending talents and skills with teammates. It's about covering for one another. Whether on an inner city street, or a dusty, pebble-covered sandlot, or under the lights at Fenway Park, the heart of the matter is the game itself: the unforgettable sound of a fastball struck solidly by a wooden bat, the up-against-the-wall, over-the-shoulder catch in the webbing of the outstretched glove, the headlong slide under the tag at third, or simply another routine grounder to short.

In 1977 I moved from Saltillo, Mexico, to Mexico City to work as a contractual assignee for the church. I was charged to work with our small congregation in the heart of one of the world's largest cities. My primary role was outreach among youth and families. I was a rookie, and the congregation was struggling. I made lots of visits, stumbled through a number of classes, stumbled over the language, erred embarrassingly in scripture and theology, but established friendships, shared special moments in the lives of special people, and slowly began to get things wrong less often.

We were a rag-tag team at times. People had personal struggles, there were economic and cultural differences, and there were family tensions that got played out in congregational life. But in the midst of this team, I had the privilege of sharing in my first two baptisms. I miscalculated distance and bumped Enrique's head on the cement font, and struggled with the baptismal prayer in Spanish before baptizing Héctor. But it was a special moment in my life and theirs, and in the life of that less-than-perfect community of faith.

When I think about the strength of our denomination, I am very proud of the caliber of competent preachers, teachers, and administrators among us. I am proud of the dreamers of an architectural marvel like the Temple, of the Messiah choir that can receive a standing ovation before the brightest and best in Carnegie Hall; proud of international worship experiences that blend music, color, words, and heritage into a Spirit-enhanced gift that glorifies God and edifies God's many peoples.

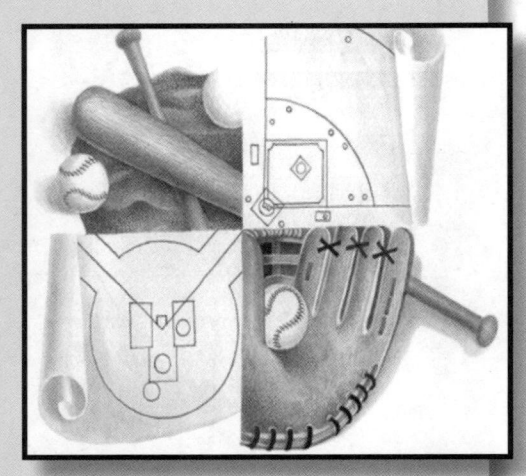

Make no mistake, friends, we are called to standards of excellence we have not yet achieved and on which we cannot compromise. We need those who can operate in the major leagues, as it were.

But that is not the measure of our joy or strength. That is not the ultimate goal we seek in our discipleship. Our strength, our life, our purpose as a people can be manifest *anywhere*. Wherever and whenever and among whomever we share the Spirit of Christ, which brings peace, reconciliation, and healing of the human spirit, there is the source and measure of our purpose as God's people. *There* is our ultimate joy.

Baseball still captures me—the artistry, the strategy, the teamwork, the competition, the hope of one more chance to join the choreographed dance of it all. Another even greater joy has also claimed me. In those *whenever, wherever* moments when Christ is shared in a way that reaches and transforms others and me, I know a captivity that frees me as nothing else can. I'm *still* ready!

[11]*Excerpts from David R. Brock "Oh, the Joy! Reflections on Baseball and Discipleship"*

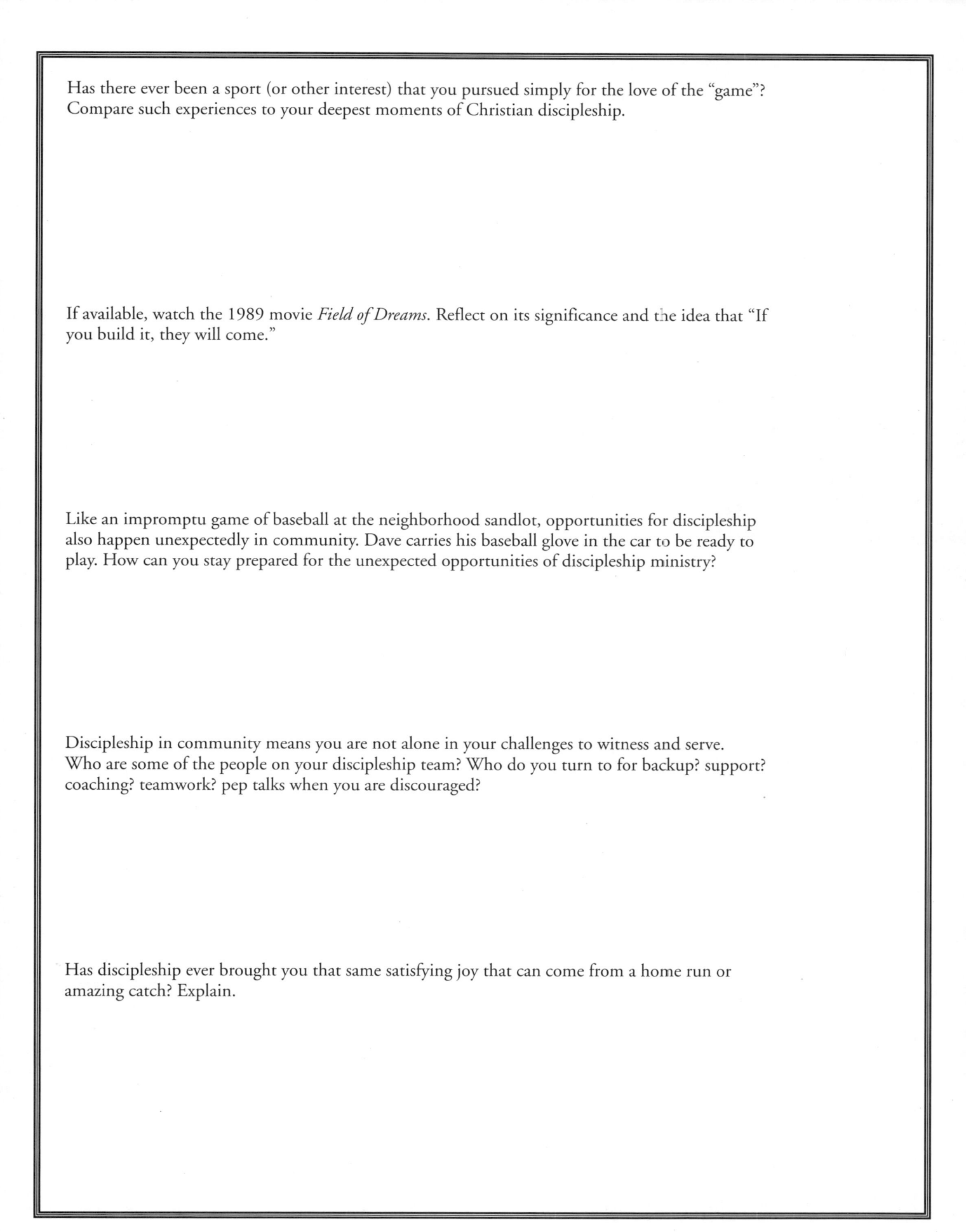

Has there ever been a sport (or other interest) that you pursued simply for the love of the "game"? Compare such experiences to your deepest moments of Christian discipleship.

If available, watch the 1989 movie *Field of Dreams*. Reflect on its significance and the idea that "If you build it, they will come."

Like an impromptu game of baseball at the neighborhood sandlot, opportunities for discipleship also happen unexpectedly in community. Dave carries his baseball glove in the car to be ready to play. How can you stay prepared for the unexpected opportunities of discipleship ministry?

Discipleship in community means you are not alone in your challenges to witness and serve. Who are some of the people on your discipleship team? Who do you turn to for backup? support? coaching? teamwork? pep talks when you are discouraged?

Has discipleship ever brought you that same satisfying joy that can come from a home run or amazing catch? Explain.

Define Community

Look up the definition of community in a dictionary.

From the earliest years of the Restoration, the goal of creating peaceful community (Zion) has been a central focus.

As a Christian, you will live out your discipleship in the environment of community.

How do you define community?

Peace and Justice

The Community of Christ is called to be a people dedicated to peace and justice.

- What areas in the world need peace?

- What does justice mean to you?

- Have you ever experienced something at school that seemed unfair? What did you do?

- Have you ever been in an argument or fight with someone else? How did it make you feel? What did you do? Did you ever resolve it?

- How should a disciple of Christ handle conflict situations?

Music Idea
"Community of Christ"
Rock Our World CD
Kevin Henrickson

My Communities

As an individual, you are a part of many different communities (family, school, church, friends, teams).

What are your communities and what part do you play in each one?

Living My Discipleship

Look at your list of personal communities. When is it hardest for you to live out your discipleship? Why do you think that is and what can you do to change it?

Community of Christ Church Seal

What will have to happen to create the kind of peaceful community described in Isaiah 11:6–7? What can you do to help?

The wolf shall live with the lamb, the leopard shall lie down with the kid, the calf and the lion and the fatling together, and a little child shall lead them.

The cow and the bear shall graze, their young shall lie down together; and the lion shall eat straw like the ox.
—Isaiah 11:6–7
NRSV

Discipleship in Community

If discipleship is carried out *in* community, then learning about it *through* community is important. Even if you are going through this study alone, gather a group of family or friends to help you work through the activities on this page.

Community Strengthens Us

Share this object lesson on community as a children's moment in a worship or with a children's class.

Give each child two small, (dry) thin sticks. Ask them to break one of their sticks in half. This should be no problem. Explain that the single sticks represent one person. Alone, we try our best, but sometimes we break. Gather the second stick from each person. Tie a string around the bundle to represent God, who loves each one. Now let each person try to break the bundle. Explain that when we work together for Christ, we are all much stronger. We can rely on one another for strength. If there are only a few in class, add more sticks to the bundle to represent parents, teachers, congregational members, neighbors, family, and friends.

Worship in Community

It is within the church community that people come together for worship.

Write the following activities on slips of paper. Choose one slip at a time and role play the activity listed (like charades). After each turn, discuss the importance of the activity in worship.
- share gifts and talents
- sing
- pray
- praise God
- preach
- sacraments
- study and learn
- give offerings
- read scripture
- visit with friends
- laugh
- share love

Take the speaker out for a meal after the service. Discuss the sermon, preparation for preaching, and discipleship through worship.

As you listen and participate, write notes or draw pictures to help you remember key points of the service. Discuss the sermon with others in your small group community.

Help plan and participate in a worship service.

Act out conflict situations that happen in your communities of school, church, family, and neighborhood. Discuss peaceful steps that can be taken in each situation.

Peaceful Resolutions

Walk in Their Shoes

high heels
dance shoes
basketball shoes
soccer shoes
dress shoes
bowling shoes
nurse's shoes
work boots
swim shoes
snow boots
fire fighter boots
fishing boots
sandals

As a disciple of Christ, Christians are called to celebrate the worth of all people, no matter where they live, what they do, what they wear, what they look like, or who their friends might be. Jesus explained it very simply: "You shall love your neighbor as yourself" (Mark 12:31 NRSV).

Provide a variety of shoes. Choose shoes that are identifiable with specific activities or characteristics.

Let each person choose a pair or shoes, try them on, walk around and model them, and then sit down. Discuss who wears the shoes and why. What part do people who wear the shoes play in the community? What unique challenges and possible needs for ministry do these people face?

Discuss the types of shoes you wear. What parts can you play in the community? What can you do to promote communities of joy, hope, love, and peace?

Session Objectives

- To understand that followers of Jesus Christ are responsible for helping others to follow him

- To learn that actions and words are the first witness of beliefs

- To recognize that all have testimonies to share

A Disciple's Call to Witness

IMAGE Reflection

8

The Courage to Be a Witness

[12] By Jared Munson... teenager, athlete, and minister

Ever since I can remember, my parents, Kathy and Jimmy, have always prayed that the grace of God would bless me, their only child, with the gift of courage. My mom said that when I was blessed as a baby the one gift they asked the elders to pray for was courage. My dad still prays that God will overwhelm me with the gift of courage.

My parents told me they could ask for wealth, wisdom, or confidence as my blessing, but instead they hope courage is the one core gift that I will take into the world. They taught me that with courage a person could have the freedom to do things out of calling, never necessity. I am not sure what this means but I am trying to learn.

At the time of writing this, I am not sure I have very much courage. I am scared of many things. But my parents have tried to teach me that courage has nothing to do with the lack of fears. Instead my dad said the more fears a person has, the more opportunity for courage they have. Courage means you are not without fear but that you face your fears. Courage means your fears never hold you back. My dad said without fear it is impossible to have courage. So if this is true, I have many opportunities to be brave because I fear many things. Maybe when you are a teenager, being afraid is uncool but so is not being honest with yourself.

What Goes Around, Comes Around

What goes around, comes around. These words have always been used in a somewhat negative sense. They have been used to teach me that what you dish out to others will eventually be dished out back to you. But in this experience, those words were God's revelation to me.

I was about nine years old, and late one night I went to the hospital with my dad to see someone. I have always enjoyed sharing with Dad as he went out to minister. You never knew what might happen. With Dad very little is ever routine. What appeared to be a routine visit to the hospital ended up becoming an experience of wonderment about God's grace.

When we were leaving to walk out to our car, we noticed a young man sitting alone in the hallway of the parking garage near the doctor's entrance. The man looked so sad.

In Dad's view, a person who is sad is the perfect missionary prospect. Somebody who is sad needs a friend. Who can be a better friend than Jesus?

So here I go walking side by side with my dad to interrupt the lonely man's sadness. Dad sat down in the chair right next to the man and began talking to him. The young man tried to ignore us and hide his tears. Dad just continued to chat. Finally Dad said to the young man, "My son, Jared, and I were heading back to our car. When we walked by you it was easy to notice you are troubled, so we just wanted to stop by to see if there was anything we could do for you."

Before long the young man was telling Dad all his secrets. He was an intern at the children's hospital. For the first time he had just seen a child patient die. He told us he was scared. He was crying lightly. The man told us he was afraid to fail.

I was just nine but I felt so bad. Dad was just sitting there. I stood up and told my dad this man needed prayer. Dad followed the lead-in and asked the man if he could pray for him. The man said yes. My dad asked me to pray for the man's fear to go away and I did. Dad then administered to the man and we left.

Since that time I have seen him at the hospital but he does not remember me. More than six years have passed since this experience. I have been ordained a priest in the Community of Christ and have been asked to join as a member of the chaplain team.

On my first day to be at the children's hospital as a chaplain, I was scared. I was so scared I was sick. I wanted to just call Dad to come and get me. I did not leave the chaplain's office. I was given a list of rooms to visit but I was just too afraid.

Then a man came in with a nametag that read "Dr. Vincent King." It was the man from my experience as a nine year old. He said, "Hello Jared. Do you remember me?" I told him that I did. He told me that he heard I was a teenage chaplain. He said he felt it was a great thing for a young man to be ordained.

I was shocked. I thought he'd forgotten me. It had been six years. Dr. King asked me if I was OK. I told him I was scared. He said, "Well, let me pray for you." He put his arm around me and prayed. He then said, "Remember when you prayed for me when I was scared? Well, *what goes around, comes around*. You will be great. Let me know if I can help you. I am glad you are here." He left the room and I found the courage to begin a new thing.

This might sound strange but I knew from this experience that Jesus was with me. The grace of God had stored away a six-year-old experience and a stranger in the night to give me strength and a new friend on a day when my courage was buried. Being a worker for Jesus is so cool. Jesus always does neat stuff!

What I Learned

I learned from this experience to be bold. No matter where we are and no matter what time it is, we need to be aware of the needs around us, even those of a stranger.

I've learned not to be afraid of making a fool of myself. I have seen Jesus bless boldness when it is sincere.

I've also learned that being afraid is a common experience and nothing to hide from. I also know Jesus understands our fear and tries to help provide us the courage to face it.

The thing I have learned most from this experience is that many times—not always—but many times when we take time out to lend a prayer or helping hand to someone else, it will come back to us when we need it the most. Serving Jesus is such a great adventure.

Look at the picture on page 48. The covered wagon is a picture of the "Gospel Waggon" used to spread the word of the gospel with Australia in the early years of the Community of Christ denomination. Where do you find opportunities to witness?

If you notice someone, a stranger, sitting alone and appearing sad, would you walk up to him or her and try to begin a conversation? Why or why not?

What would you say to a medical professional who just saw their first patient die?

How would you respond to a friend who has lost someone to death?

Jared experienced a response to his ministry six years after his contact with the doctor. More often than not, as you put yourself "out there" for God, you will have no knowledge of how the people you have witnessed to respond. What do you need to keep you witnessing?

Witnessing or ministering? Is there a difference and if so, what is it? Do you want to witness, minister, or both? Why?

The Great Commission

The great commission to proclaim the gospel and make disciples in all the world finds its model in the ministry of Jesus.

Look up each scripture, then record the way Jesus witnessed. Next, take that example and identify a specific situation where you can use the same model to witness to people in your community.

> Now the eleven disciples went to Galilee, to the mountain to which Jesus had directed them. When they saw him, they worshiped him; but some doubted. And Jesus came and said to them, "All authority in heaven and on earth has been given to me. Go therefore and make disciples of all nations, baptizing them in the name of the Father and of the Son and of the Holy Spirit, and teaching them to obey everything that I have commanded you. And remember, I am with you always, to the end of the age."—Matthew 28:16–20 NRSV

Jesus Did . . .   I Can . . .

- Matthew 9:9–13

- Matthew 18:21–22

- Mark 4:1–9, 33–34

- Mark 10:13–16

- Luke 19:1–10

- John 4:7–19, 39–42

- John 8:1–11

You've heard the saying, "actions speak louder than words." When it comes to sharing your witness as a disciple of Christ, nothing is more true!

Unwritten Messages

Following are some common situations in which our witness through actions may be tested. For each situation described, list one response that expresses a negative witness and an alternative response that would expresses a positive witness. What is different about the witness each response portrays?

- Someone cuts in front of you in line for a movie you've been waiting an hour to see.

- You are driving friends to school when another driver runs a red light, causing you to swerve, barely missing a serious accident.

- You are choosing a T-shirt to wear to a concert with your friends.

- You are choosing a movie to watch with younger children.

- You are angry at a teacher for what you believe is an unfair grade.

- Even though you are underage, your friends offer to get you into the hottest bar in town.

- Your parents embarrass you in front of others.

- You work at a local restaurant. While waiting tables, a customer is very rude.

- You find yourself jealous of the date your old girlfriend (boyfriend) brings to the court-warming dance.

- The kids you are hanging out with continually make fun of the student who speaks with a significant stutter.

A common trend today is license plates that carry a personal message. Create messages on the plates that would share a positive witness of God's message for everyone.

License-Plate Witness

A Way to Begin

A disciple's witness happens everyday, everywhere, but stepping out to deliberately witness can be scary. A little evaluation and planning can help as you begin.

Take an honest look at yourself and your communities to create a beginning plan for witnessing.

How has Christ made a difference in your life?

Where do teens in your community gather?

What problems face teens in your community?

What is the gospel message you want others to understand?

What are your strengths? *(Look at the Ministry Tool List on page 36.)*

Who was the first person to tell you about the gospel of Christ?

testimony
+
strengths
+
people
+
places
+
opportunities
=
witness plan

> You are the light of the world. A city built on a hill cannot be hid. No one after lighting a lamp puts it under the bushel basket, but on the lampstand, and it gives light to all in the house. In the same way, let your light shine before others, so that they may see your good works and give glory to [God] in heaven.
> —Matthew 5:14–16 NRSV adapted

Each One, Reach One

Each one, reach one—a simple challenge with a powerful impact. Image how many people would be brought to the knowledge of Christ if each person in the church shared their witness with just one other person! And if that person shares their witness? You do the math!

3 Three people I will witness to are:

How I can show them God's love:

Session Objectives

- To acknowledge a personal journey of experiences and people

- To find ways to renew, refuel, and refocus

- To use Section 161 as a guide to discipleship

- To examine the personal commitment of baptism

Deepening the Journey

IMAGE Reflection

9

Expressway of the Disciple

This past January I was heading into Chicago for an 8:30 a.m. meeting. I live in Naperville, Illinois, a suburb about thirty-five miles west of the city. I left my house at 7:00 a.m. to get to the Naperville train station by 7:28. The express train got to the city in about thirty-five minutes. I walked through busy Union Station out to the bus stop, and waited twenty minutes. The bus was late. I squeezed onto a seat and proceeded to bounce around through the stops and the shifting of bodies of every size, shape, and color. Another fifteen minutes on the crowded bus and I reached my destination. I stumbled to my seat and collapsed somewhat exhausted before the meeting even began.

After my commute I took a deep breath and thought to myself, You really have to be tough and somewhat intense to survive and thrive in an urban setting. The same could be said at times for traveling the path of the disciple.

In an urban setting, the path is not a rocky trail that winds through a meadow or around a beautiful mountain, the path is one that leads you down roaring interstates, or along rail lines, or busy city streets. This path is not serene, where you can take time to meditate and listen to the quiet sounds of birds chirping or the wind whistling through the trees. This path is complex, alive with people, rhythms, danger, energy, and adventure.

A call to reconciliation, justice, learning, sharing, spirituality, and community isn't any easier many times than my commute to Chicago. You can look at the challenges along the way as barriers or gifts. It is unbelievably difficult to not become entangled on the path, to not let negative attitudes and conflict drag you down. But during those moments when you don't allow the path to consume you, it can teach you. It is much like my friend Paul Davis referenced in his February *Herald* article "The Path to Discipleship": "To walk a path is to give yourself to the path, to let the path tell you where to place your next step."

When I missed a bus one evening after a late meeting, I started to tense up. I knew missing the bus meant I would miss the train and I would get home an hour later than I had planned. For some reason this time instead of becoming frustrated I decided to "give myself to the path." I began to walk the thirteen blocks to the train station. Along the way an African-American woman, whom I assumed was homeless, walked up beside me and asked if she could walk with me to the train. I love to visit with people, so this was perfectly fine with me. She showed me that she was wearing several pairs of pants and several sweatshirts. I knew this conversation would eventually lead her to asking me for money, but we continued to walk and talk. She shared with me how she became homeless. Several years earlier she had run down the street from her house to buy cigarettes and left her four-year-old daughter home alone. A fire swept through her home, killing her child, and leaving her in total despair. She turned to drugs, and her life spiraled downward.

After sharing her story, she turned to me and I anticipated this would be the time she requested money, but she didn't. She said God had found her in the midst of the chaos and she was now embracing all the gifts around her. She urged me to do the same. She said, "Be thankful for everything." When we arrived at the station I invited her in; I said I would buy her something to eat. She said no, but asked if we could hold hands and on the count of three yell in praise to God and in thanks for our brief relationship. After hesitating momentarily I agreed. There I stood in a business suit, with a briefcase, holding hands with a ragged, tattooed, pierced, beautiful woman, yelling at the top of my lungs. It was amazing. She left without taking a dime and I left with an entire treasure.

I have often thought about that brief interaction and the experience of looking into the face of Christ, and I am reminded that the city, often thought of as a place of despair and oppression, is resplendent in gifts. God had found me, even on a busy Chicago street. This meeting along the path had reminded me about the importance of justice, community, spirituality, sharing, reconciliation, and truly understanding the message of the gospel.

God can find you on the path—sometimes in the silence when you are listening intently and other times in the midst of noise, people, buildings, and that beautiful chaos.

Embrace the journey!

[13] *Susan Cochran*

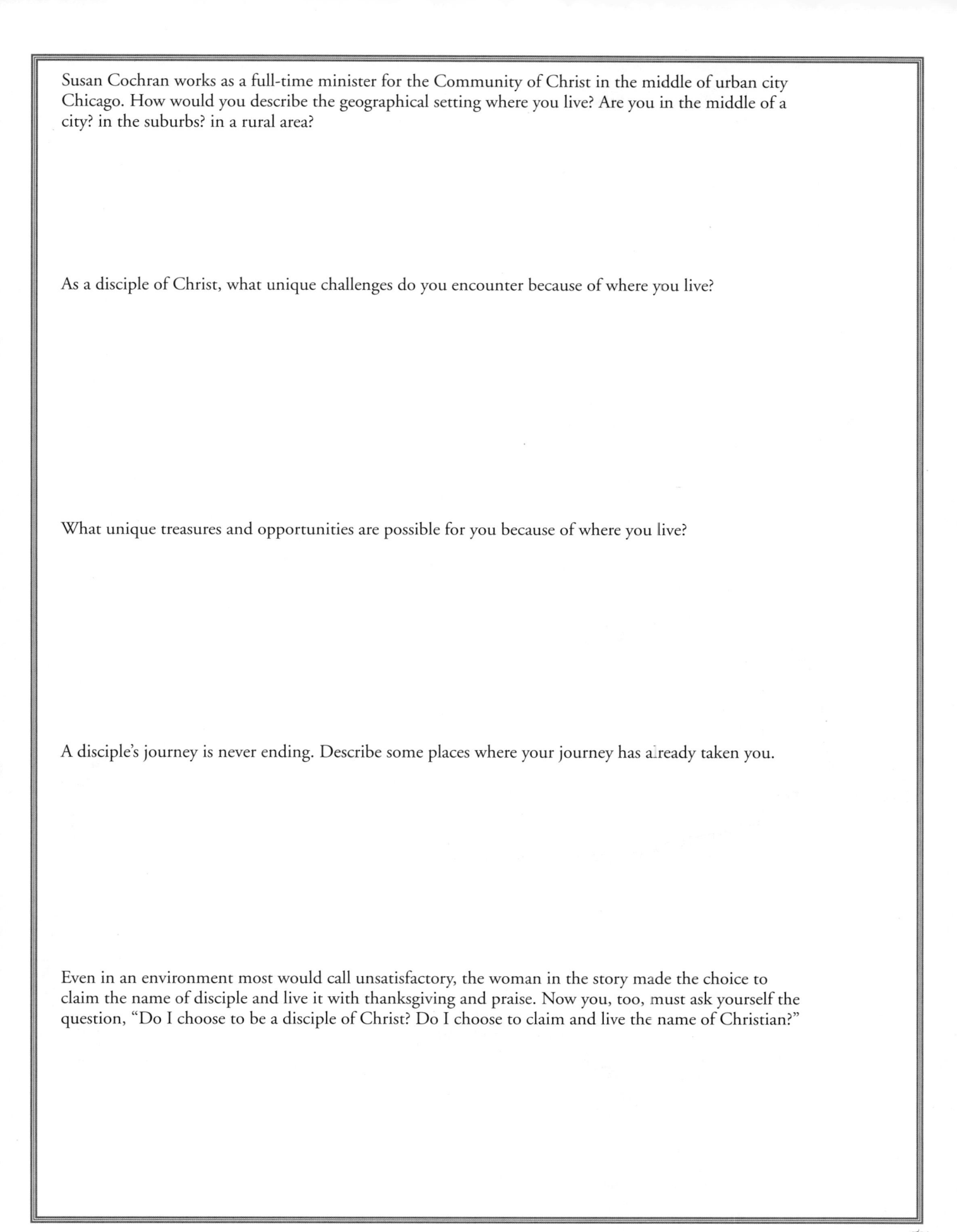

Susan Cochran works as a full-time minister for the Community of Christ in the middle of urban city Chicago. How would you describe the geographical setting where you live? Are you in the middle of a city? in the suburbs? in a rural area?

As a disciple of Christ, what unique challenges do you encounter because of where you live?

What unique treasures and opportunities are possible for you because of where you live?

A disciple's journey is never ending. Describe some places where your journey has already taken you.

Even in an environment most would call unsatisfactory, the woman in the story made the choice to claim the name of disciple and live it with thanksgiving and praise. Now you, too, must ask yourself the question, "Do I choose to be a disciple of Christ? Do I choose to claim and live the name of Christian?"

Celebrate the Journey

Create a map of the journey that has brought you to this place in your relationship with God. Answer the questions. Are there other people and places you should recognize along the way?

Life's journey places before you a banquet of experiences and choices, people and places. Within each is opportunity for you to learn, to serve, and to grow in your discipleship.

- Childhood friends:
- My favorite teachers:
- Someone who taught me about faith:
- Places I have worked:
- A camp counselor I remember:
- Places I have gone to school:
- Family members who have influenced my life:
- First place I heard about Jesus:
- Places I have traveled:
- A time when I questioned God:
- People I know who are of a different race or culture:
- Someone who cared:
- Places I have lived:
- A youth leader who cared:
- A skill I have developed:
- Someone who always makes me laugh:
- A time when I believed:
- A person who lives the example of Christ for me:
- Someone who has taught me about wisdom:
- A place where I go to find God:
- A joyful memory:
- A sad memory:
- A day I made a difference:
- Someone I trust:
- A time when I was forgiven:
- A time when I forgave another:
- My name is:
- A time when I felt the Holy Spirit:
- A time when I was able to minister:
- Someone who loves me:
- A time when I knew God was real:
- and I am a child of God!
- My Community of Christ congregational family:

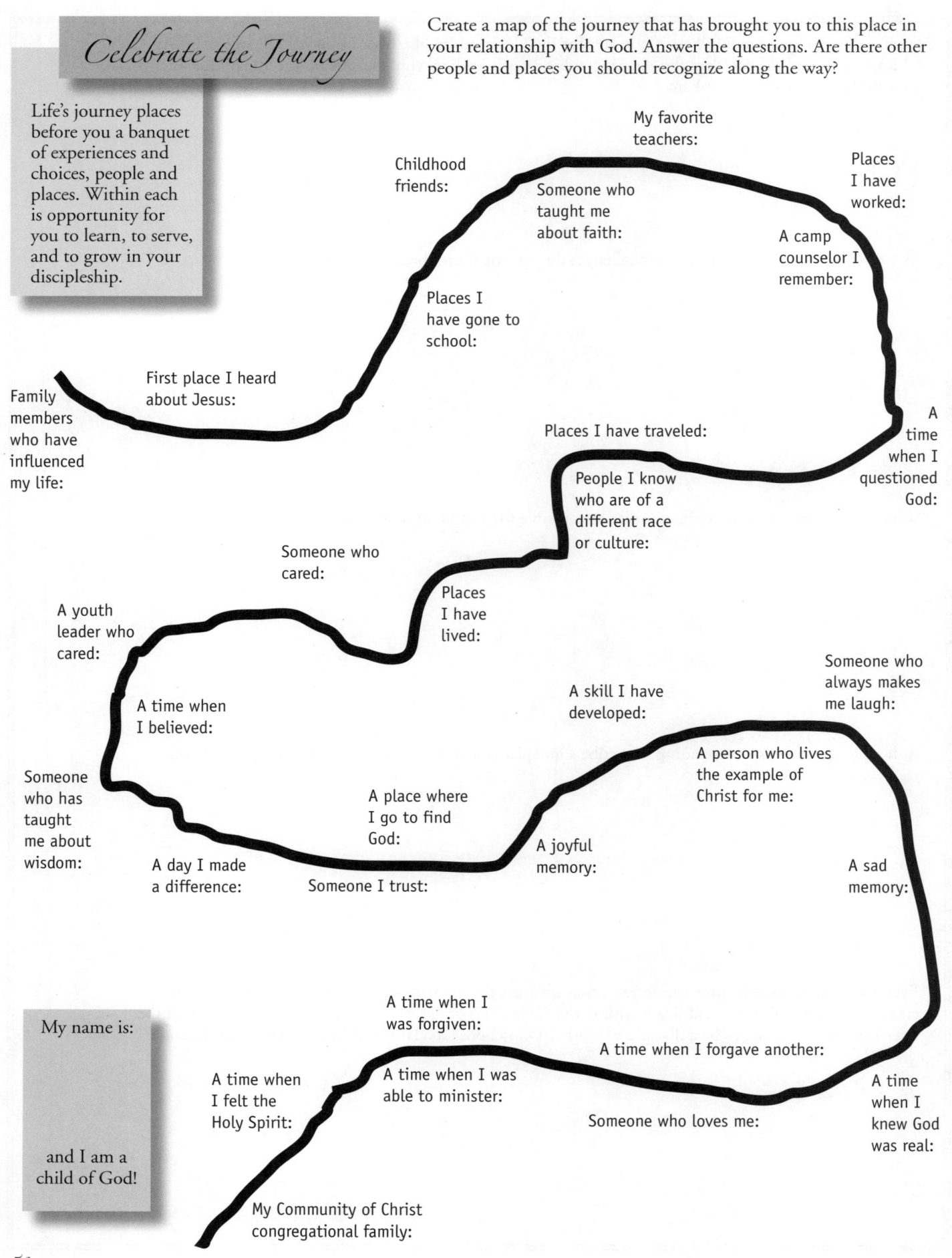

58

Renew, Refuel, Refocus

Sometimes the discipleship journey can be exhausting. To keep from getting there, take time to renew, refuel, and refocus.

Decide how you can work these energy-fueling activities into your life on a regular basis.

Share with your mentor and at least one other person what you will do.

- Read the scriptures.
- Pray—talk with God.
- Listen.
- Meditate—find time to just be.
- Seek balance.
- Worship.
- Experience nature.
- Learn about other cultures, religions, beliefs.
- Forgive.
- Accept that God loves you unconditionally.
- Listen to the testimonies of others.
- Spend time in service to others.
- Share your testimony.
- Gain strength from those who support your ministry.
- Be creative—mix things up a bit.
- Stay open to fresh ideas and opportunities.
- Keep a journal.

A Guide for Your Journey: Doctrine and Covenants 161

- Highlight the instructions for discipleship found in Section 161.
- What does this say to you and how does it relate to your discipleship journey?

1a. Lift up your eyes and fix them on the place beyond the horizon to which you are sent. Journey in trust, assured that the great and marvelous work is for this time and for all time.

b. Claim your unique and sacred place within the circle of those who call upon the name of Jesus Christ. Be faithful to the spirit of the Restoration, mindful that it is a spirit of adventure, openness, and searching. Walk proudly and with a quickened step. Be a joyful people. Laugh and play and sing, embodying the hope and freedom of the gospel.

2a. Become a people of the Temple—those who see violence but proclaim peace, who feel conflict yet extend the hand of reconciliation, who encounter broken spirits and find pathways for healing.

b. Fulfill the purposes of the Temple by making its ministries manifest in your hearts. It was built from your sacrifices and searching over many generations. Let it stand as a towering symbol of a people who knew injustice and strife on the frontier and who now seek the peace of Jesus Christ throughout the world.

3a. Open your hearts and feel the yearning so your brothers and sisters who are lonely, despised, fearful, neglected, unloved. Reach out in understanding, clasp their hands, and invite all to share in the blessings of community created in the name of the One who suffered for all.

b. Do not be fearful of one another. Respect each life journey, even in its brokenness and uncertainty, for each person has walked alone at times. Be ready to listen and slow to criticize, lest judgments be unrighteous and unredemptive.

c. Be patient with one another, for creating sacred community is arduous and even painful. But it is to loving community such as this that each is called. Be courageous and visionary, believing in the power of just a few vibrant witnesses to transform the world. Be assured that love will overcome the voices of fear, division, and deceit.

d. Understand that the road to transformation travels both inward and outward. The road to transformation is the path of the disciple.

4a. Do not neglect the smallest among you, for even the least of these are treasures in God's sight. Receive the giftedness and energy of children and youth, listening to understand their questions and their wisdom. Respond to their need to be loved and nurtured as they grow.

b. Be mindful of the changing of life's seasons, of the passage from the springtime of childhood and youth to the winter years of life. Embrace the blessing of your many differences. Be tender and caring. Be reminded once again that the gifts of all are necessary in order that divine purposes may be accomplished.

5 Be respectful of tradition. Do not fail to listen attentively to the telling of the sacred story, for the story of scripture and of faith empowers and illuminates. But neither be captive to time-bound formulas and procedures. Remember that instruction given in former years is applicable in principle and must be measured against the needs of a growing church, in accordance with the prayerful direction of the spiritual authorities and the consent of the people.

6a. Stand firm in the name of the One you proclaim and create diverse communities of disciples and seekers, rejoicing in the continuing fulfillment of the call to this people to prophetically witness in the name of Jesus Christ.

b. Heed the urgent call to become a global family united in the name of the Christ, committed in love to one another, seeking the kingdom for which you yearn and to which you have always been summoned. That kingdom shall be a peaceable one and it shall be known as Zion.

7 The Spirit of the One you follow is the spirit of love and peace. That Spirit seeks to abide in the hearts of those who would embrace its call and live its message. The path will not always be easy, the choices will not always be clear, but the cause is sure and the Spirit will bear witness to the truth, and those who live the truth will know the hope and the joy of discipleship in the community of Christ. Amen.

Do You Want to Be Baptized?

1. Pray about your decision, then discuss it with your mentor, pastor, and parents.

2. Ask a priest or elder to baptize you.

3. Ask two elders to confirm you.

4. Speak with your pastor and/or worship planner to schedule a date.

5. Help plan the service.

6. Make a list of people you want to invite to the service, then invite them. Be sure to send invitations to your unchurched friends—what a great witness!

Endnotes

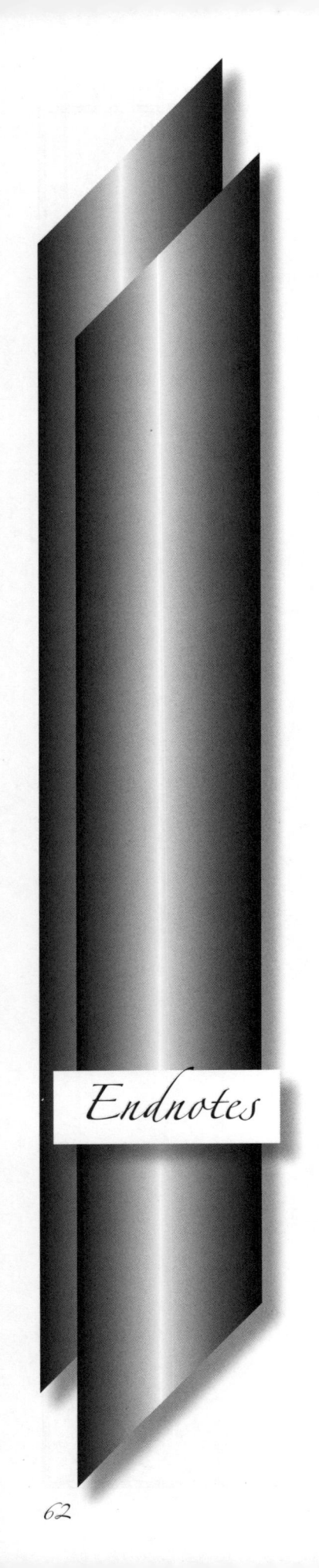

1. Carolyn Brock, *Called by a New Name* (Independence: Herald House, 2001), 3–4.
2. Dale Luffman, "An Account of God: A Trinitarian Reflection," *The Knowledge of God*, TE 252 (Independence: Community of Christ Temple School), 79f.
3. Elizabeth A. Johnson, "Trinity: To Let the Symbol Sing Again," *Theology Today* (Vol 54, No 3):299–311.
4. Jung Young Lee, *The Trinity in Asian Perspective* (Nashville: Abingdon Press, 1996), 15.
5. Anthony Chvala-Smith and Charmaine Chvala-Smith "A Becoming Faith—Wondering on the Way," *Herald* (July 2001): 8.
6. *Claim the Name: Confirmation Teaching Plans for 39 Weeks* (Nashville: Abingdon Press, 2000), 155.
7. W. Grant McMurray, "Celebrate Our Story: Heritage as a Resource for the Future," *Herald* (September 2001): 17–21.
8. *Seekers and Disciples* (Independence: Herald House, 2001), 35–46.
9. New International Version Youth Devotional Bible (Grand Rapids: Zondervan), 1247.
10. *Tithing: A Disciple's Generous Response* (Independence: Herald House, 2002): 6–9.
11. David R. Brock, "Oh, the Joy! Reflections on Baseball and Discipleship," *Herald* (November 2002): 11–13.
12. Jared Munson, *Courageous Witness: A Teenager Shares Jesus* (Independence: Herald House, 2003).
13. Susan Cochran, "Expressway of the Disciple,"*Herald* (August 2002): 8.

▶ Why did you study this resource?

- ○ to prepare for baptism
- ○ to deepen my discipleship journey
- ○ other _____

▶ How did you study this resource?
- ○ as a small informal group with mentor
- ○ as a family
- ○ as an individual with a mentor
- ○ camp or retreat setting
- ○ class setting with a teacher
- ○ other _____

▶ On a scale of one to five, how would you rate the usefulness of this resource?

poor   good   excellent
1   2   3   4   5

▶ What sections of this resource did you find most helpful?

- ○ God, Jesus, and the Holy Spirit
- ○ Scriptures of the Church
- ○ Community of Christ: Then and Now
- ○ Church Sacraments
- ○ Called to Serve the Lord
- ○ A Disciple's Generous Response
- ○ Discipleship in Community
- ○ A Disciple's Call to Witness
- ○ Deepening the Journey

✓ check all that apply

▶ In future resources of this kind, what would you like to see changed?

▶ What follow-up resources would be helpful for you?

▶ Comments and suggestions:

▼ Your age? _____

Was this resource appropriate for your age?

- ○ Yes
- ○ No

Of Water and Spirit
Deepening the Journey
Evaluation

Return this evaluation to

Community of Christ
Forefront Ministries
1001 W. Walnut
Independence, MO
64050-3562

place stamp here

Community of Christ

Forefront Ministries
1001 W. Walnut
Independence, MO 64050-3562

- - - - - - - - - - - - - - - - -

Fold in half and tape closed to mail.